MONEY

A SIMPLE WAY TO CREATE ABUNDANCE

MATTHEW GROS-WERTER

First published in 2024
by
Matthew Gros-Werter
www.matthewgw.com
112 Bowery, New York, NY 10013

Text copyright © 2024
Matthew Gros-Werter

Editor: Ariel Gros-Werter

Art Direction & Design: 16B Studio

Library of Congress Cataloging-in-Publication Data
Matthew Gros-Werter
Money, A Simple Way to Create Abundance

INCLUDES INDEX.
PAPERBACK ISBN: 9798884673496

ALL RIGHTS RESERVED
PRINTED IN THE UNITED STATES OF AMERICA

No part of this publication may be reproduced or used in any form or by any means — graphic, electronic, or mechanical, including photocopying, recording, taping, or information-storage and retrieval systems — without written permission from the author Matthew Gros-Werter.

Books are available at special discounts when purchased in bulk for premiums and sales promotions, as well as for fundraising or educational use.

Imprint: Independently published
Special editions or book excerpts can be created to specification.

For details, please contact the Special Sales Director at the address above.

FIRST PRINTING, 2024
1 2 3 4 5 6 7 8 9 / 15 14 13 12 11 10 09 08 07

I want to thank my mom and dad
for their support throughout the years.

Special thanks to my sister Ariel
who edited this book.

In loving memory of my grandmother who pushed me to try my best every day.

**In loving memory of Greg
who saw greatness in me before I could.**

MONEY

A SIMPLE WAY
TO CREATE
ABUNDANCE

TABLE OF CONTENTS:

	Forward	9
1.	Introduction - Why I Wrote this Book	13
2.	Money I - The Usefulness of Money	17
3.	About Me - My story	21
4.	Perseverance - Your Inner Power	29
5.	Meditation	33
	a. Awareness of Your Beliefs	
	b. The Meditation	
6.	Language and Gratitude	51
	a. Changing Beliefs	
	b. It's the Little Things That Count	
7.	Money II - What is it?	65
8.	Laws of the Universe	73
	Understanding How the Universe Can Support You	
9.	Manifestation - Calling in Your Future	87
10.	Plan - Creating Action Steps Towards Your Success	93
11.	Minimums - How to Stay Motivated	99
12.	Perfection - It's Not What You Think	111
13.	Change - The Only Constant	115
14.	Afterthought - The Best Project	121
	Appendix	127

FORWARD

In the early 2010s, I was leading a weekly Meditation at a community center in New York City. One day Matthew Gros-Werter came to one of my Meditations. It was a delightful surprise as I had known Matthew nearly his entire life, being friends with his parents. What Matthew hadn't known was that I was a longtime meditator, at that time for almost 40 years, having studied Meditation at ashrams here in the U.S. and in India, starting in my late-20s.

After the Meditation, Matthew told me why he had started meditating daily a few years earlier, to manage painful headaches. The headaches had since gone away, which he attributed to his meditation practice. Now that his initial reasons for meditating were resolved, and he felt a new sense of awareness setting in, he was eager, curious, and excited to learn more about deepening his practice.

We began having regular dialogues about Meditation and spiritual life. Matthew has had a lot of questions as well as many realizations on the use of meditation, including:

How can meditation help us uplift our daily lives?
How do we bring more meaning and purpose into our relationships and work lives?
How do we manifest more of what we want in life and out of life?

These are among the searing questions Matthew explores in this book.

A serious student of meditation and spiritual seeker, Matthew recounts bringing the fruits of his contemplative practice into the business world. Sharing meditative practices and insights, he offers accessible and down-to-earth advice for personal growth that at first glance might seem abstract or esoteric, but is actually quite practical.

One example is learning to leverage our awareness of our own beliefs to change those beliefs. Another is creating an action plan for personal success and manifestation.

Ultimately, Matthew shares his meditation journey from stress and pain to contemplation -- looking at his own mind, as a way of deepening his awareness and expanding his accountability to himself and to others. His goal is to inspire others along the path to self-awareness and contentment.

Sheldon Lewis

Mind-Body Practitioner and Meditation Teacher, New York City

1.
INTRODUCTION

"Don't let the fear of striking out hold you back."

–Babe Ruth

When I first was asked to write this book, I was a bit confused why. I have great knowledge of business, yes; I've consulted for companies and helped friends build their businesses, yes; I have my own unique ideas relating to money and business, yes; I'm the type of guy who likes to analyze ideas to get more clarity as to best practices, yes. But more than that, I overcame the pain of not believing in myself and developed myself into a spiritual businessman. I have a 10-year strong daily meditation practice, am deeply spiritual and am humbled by the human experience.

I grappled how to present my ideas about business and spirituality in a way that would let you, the reader, start at one place and by the end have more self-confidence, more self-awareness, more certainty and more tools to either start or grow a business or get a promotion or a new job.

Those who work for me know I have always taken big picture ideas and broken them down into bite size action steps which each can be explained in a few minutes. I realized early on that when leading, it's important to get my team moving and trying things, allowing them to create their own methods and styles. I'd give them ideas and information that they could tweak to make sense of for themselves. My challenge in writing this book was how to take big ideas and simplify them so readers can move onto action steps quickly, to develop methods that work for them.

The first third of this book is filled with meditation and healing modalities to find your inner self, identify your strengths, and build your confidence. To grow your inner awareness and break down negative inner dialogue so you can succeed. The middle portion is a discussion on money and how to use the laws of the universe to attract it through manifestation. The last third are business practices to start or grow a business or get a job or a promotion. Once you start the action steps, you will be guided how to stay motivated - a method so powerful that you will not only appreciate your productivity, you'll have fun with your work. Work will become enjoyable and easy.

This book is laid out as a workbook. All of the concepts and ideas presented are tried-and-tested and work. These are the concepts and ideas I share with my team to develop them and make them successful. These ideas give my team, and will give you, an arsenal of tools to work with and utilize when necessary. So it is best to start at the beginning and work your way through the book. Even if you think you know the concept or idea being discussed, I assure you the way I present it will be different and more engaging. There is self-work for you to do in each chapter to help boost you in your development. You'll get the best results by grabbing a notebook and doing the self-work.

Lastly, have fun in this experience. This book is designed to make you more confident, more self-aware and more powerful. There are no right or wrong answers for your self-work, it is just for you. You may choose to do the self-work only once, that's fine. You may want to go back to it at a later point and see what has changed in you. You'll find you have new awareness and a new insight of yourself and your business, and that your answers will be different than when you first started. I enjoy looking back at my old thoughts and beliefs to see how far I've grown.

I'm excited for you to undertake this journey of self-growth. I wish you the best of luck, success, happiness and joy. This process is all about you and I'm happy to share with you the knowledge I have acquired so you too can realize your potential.

SELF WORK: Find the song "Eye of the Tiger" (from the movie "Rocky") on YouTube or a streaming service and play it. I recommend standing while listening. You may want to move to the music, shake, bounce, punch the air... anything goes! Or you may want to do nothing at all and just listen. All are good options. Have fun with it.

2.
THE USEFULNESS OF MONEY

"Money makes the world go around
It makes the world go 'round.

A mark, a yen, a buck,
or a pound
A buck or a pound
A buck or a pound
Is all that makes the world
go around,
That clinking clanking sound
Can make the world go 'round."

–Cabaret, 1972

As a child, I used to love watching old movies that glamorized wealthy lifestyles. The mansions, fancy parties, tuxedos and ball gowns, chauffeured cars and champagne. These were images of Hollywood at its best and I loved imagining what it would be like to be part of that glamor and wealth. It was very exciting.

One of my favorite displays of the excitement of money is from the movie "Cabaret." In a song titled "Money makes the world go round," Liza Minelli and her co-star, Joel Grey, play entertainers at the Kit Kat Club in Berlin and dance around the stage, tossing coins, shaking their money makers, poking fun and showing their desire for money. It is a satirical look at how important money is to life, and is a lot of fun to watch.

Think about the significance of money: money is good, money is bad. Money gives freedom. We love money, we fear the power of money. Money is excitement. Money is greed, money can be humbling. Our emotions around money run deep. Regardless of how we look at it though, money is just a tool; a tool that influences us and allows us to operate.

We use money to pay rent, to buy food and clothes, to purchase gifts, to pay doctors' bills, to be able to go out for dinner… the list goes on. The point is we use money for lots of different things. It is a necessary thing to have.

We also receive money for work we do. And it is this topic that this book is most interested in: how your beliefs around money and value affect how much you receive. Value has always been important. Before money, there was a bartering system; people would bring their crops, livestock and services to the market and trade them for other goods and services.

In our modern era, we are still trading, this time it's energy and skills for money. It is by understanding our value and what we bring to the table that we can increase the amount of money we receive for them.

SELF WORK: Write about your skills. Make this an inclusive list, not just your skill set from work. Think about both hard (technical) and soft (social) skills; include all skills you have learned in and outside of work. These are all things you bring to the table.

3.
MY STORY

"For what it's worth: it's never too late to be whoever you want to be. I hope you live a life you're proud of, and if you find you're not, I hope you have the strength to start over again."

– F. Scott Fitzgerald

There's a phrase "overnight success, 20 years in the making". While my "success" is celebrated, what is more interesting are all the things that needed to be done and evaluated to get there. All the trials, failures, restarts, thought processes, and realizations which led to awareness, perspective and my ultimate breakthrough.

My relationship with money started at the age of 7. My grandparents were having a party at their house and I helped by passing out drinks and finger food. A few weeks later I received an envelope in the mail with a thank you note from my grandfather and $7 for my services.

Wow, $7! I showed my mother. And we went to a local bank and opened a bank account designed for kids. Slowly I'd add a little money at a time to this account.

What I learned that day was money could be received. I liked the feeling of doing and receiving payment. I loved to cook and at the age of 14 I started helping a caterer on the weekends, thinking I'd be a great chef one day.

Like everyone else, I had dreams of my future. I worked towards those dreams. I read the Wall Street Journal every day on my way to high school. In college, I studied business and worked a side job, all with an eye towards my future plans. I took game theory, knowing it would help me negotiate deals. I partnered with a friend on a website that became so popular the server crashed. I helped another friend launch a clothing line.
I studied lots of business case studies and tried to learn as much as possible.

After graduating, I joined the media arm of a publishing house in late 2006. Two years later the 2008 recession set in and I was laid off. I bounced around several jobs. Someone noticed my hustle and offered me a job in technology sales. I was hungry to make a name for myself so I took it.

Especially at that time, deals that should have taken 3 months to close dragged on... and on... then they'd tell me it wasn't in the budget and the deal would never close. It was mid-recession and no one was buying.

A friend of mine had gotten into real estate brokerage and was doing pretty well. I asked if I could join him, he said yes and I got my license. My first year was a challenge - I needed to learn about creating relationships and how to work and serve clients. So I went to a sales training course taught by Greg Young, a veteran in real estate who had helped a lot of agents become successful. His course was so powerful that my deal flow doubled. I got more referrals and bigger transactions.

Greg considered me one of his guys and we often got together after work. He was a tall guy who looked a bit like John Candy, had an excellent sense of dry humor, and was brilliant. He knew how to connect with agents and make them better by inspiring them to believe in themselves. He shared with me secrets about how to motivate oneself. My business started to expand. I was arriving. My second year, one of the properties I sold was a large penthouse!

What was not apparent at the time, but has become clear to me since, was how spiritual Greg was. He and I would be at a bar and he would talk about his experience with reiki, he'd rub his hands together, feel the energy between them and say "there is a lot of power here". He had dealt with bouts of depression throughout his life and these were his medicine: beer and reiki. He used phrases and ideas that I had never heard before: authentic relationships, being genuinely happy for clients. For him it wasn't just about getting a paycheck, it was about providing a service to give people a home. When we talked about business growth he'd always say I needed to shine a light on my work to actually see what I was doing and not pretend I knew. I was inadvertently running my business in a spiritual way. During this time I started meditating (to be discussed in chapter 5) and doing yoga in order to relax and get clarity.

A few years later, Greg unfortunately had a fatal stroke. My world turned upside down. With my mentor gone, I lost focus. I lost that drive and attention to deal-making.

After 2 years of unsuccessfully trying quick-fixes to energize me, one day I walked through that "door" to the spiritual world: I started to look at my beliefs about myself, about how I interacted in business with my clients and about how I interacted with the world. I started writing them down to consider if they served me or not. I got to the core of it. I started doing the "work" to heal and grow.

I asked myself a lot of questions. Why did I believe this? What was I telling myself? What were my stories about myself? Why did I believe them? How did I feel about myself? I knew I could do more, so what was getting in my way? I needed to work on changing the beliefs and ideas that were stopping me. I started to read books about meditation, Mindfulness, the human experience and connection, as well as sales techniques and business strategies. I hired a business coach who introduced me to the law of attraction – that how we live determines what we attract. We worked to develop me to attract the type of clients I wanted. I needed to see myself differently. So I tried lots of things and took note of what worked. I wanted to become version 2.0 of me. It was going to take patience and focus, but my dreams were once again filled with success, opportunity and joy.

I looked at my values and the type of person I wanted to be. I began to develop myself into that person and acquire the characteristics I wanted to embody. I rethought how to work with clients, how to be more aligned with them, how to be of service to them rather than having them serve me, how to cooperate with them instead of only working for a paycheck. I realized business concepts integrating spiritual principles that made me faster, stronger, and more aware. Concepts and ideas which you will find in this book.

I started to trust the universe. I noticed that when I let go of holding control, things got better. When things weren't going as planned, I could believe everything was going to work out. I started to realize how little control I actually had. It was a humbling experience.

All of a sudden, the upward climb towards the figurative summit of success got easier. I was changing. I was happier. I was letting go of things that no longer served me and as a result my business changed for the better too. I acquired better clients and built better relationships. The work became fun again. This time I was on a solid foundation and I got into the state of flow. Now I own multiple companies and am a partner of other businesses. I have a strong daily spiritual practice which includes meditation, writing, speaking with others and mantras. I have awareness. I have a great life. And I mentor others to help them achieve their own success.

I could keep talking about myself, but this is not about me. This book is about you and your growth and change. I learned a lot through my hard times, and maybe you can learn from them so you won't have to struggle through it. I tried a lot of things, some worked, many didn't. I learned to ask for help when I needed it. I grew into someone I respect, like and am proud of. That's what I wish for you, to respect, like and be proud of yourself. And... you should already be, because you are on the journey to self-awareness. Remember that it is the journey that counts, the end is just the cherry on top.

I wish you all the success and happiness in the world.

SELF WORK: Write your story. Write where you started, what has been going on and what you would like to see happen.

4.
PERSEVERANCE

"Each human being is bred with a unique set of potentials that yearn to be fulfilled as surely as the acorn yearns to become the oak within it."

– Aristotle

Before we get into this book and the work, I want to congratulate you for taking the initiative to better yourself, taking the time to grow and work on your skills. You are an incredibly powerful person, you have greatness within you, you are able to persevere and push forward, get stronger, fall, dust yourself off and try again. You have so much power within you. You may not see it or may have forgotten. But I know it and I hope that you will start to see that power in yourself as well, to see what you can accomplish and know your power.

You might be thinking. "Matthew, you don't even know me. Stop filling me with hot air!"

I know you are strong. Let me explain.

Have you ever done something that was really hard and broke through and persevered? Think about it, what was that thing? You tried, failed, tried again, failed, tried again… maybe this took a while. Then one day you got it. It all became clear and you were able to do it easily. What was that thing? What did you have to overcome? How hard was it to do? How many times did you try? How badly did you want it? Did you dust yourself off quickly to try again? Did you take a break before trying again? What did it feel like when you broke through? How did it change your life? What were you able to accomplish with this newfound skill?

In case you can't think of anything I'll give an example from your life when you tried and failed and tried again until you succeeded. And once you succeeded you were a new victorious person.

It takes a baby hundreds, if not thousands, of tries until they are able to walk. Wow! Incredible! You probably don't remember, but the people around you do. They remember the first time you stood up then fell on your butt. When you were holding onto a wall or a piece of furniture to balance, then you fell again. When you finally were able to take a few steps, before you fell yet again. Again and again and again, you tried, fell on your butt, shed a few tears perhaps, got up, refocused, then tried and tried again. You had a new understanding each time you tried. How to balance, how to move one foot in front of the other. You knew you could accomplish the task. You knew you were going to get really good at walking, an expert. And everyone was cheering you on, so excited to see you succeed.

And eventually after months and months of practice, trying and falling, you let go of the support, the furniture, the push toy, the grown-ups hand and walked across the room. You were victorious and you knew it. You knew the power inside of you, proven by your newfound skill. And you were ready to unleash it on the world.

Little did your family know that you would use this newfound power to go anywhere you wanted. Perhaps, as I did, to cause a little bit of havoc and some disappearing acts – that's a story for another time.

Know that you have incredible power within you. Know that you have already accomplished incredible acts. You have come so far. Think of all the challenges that you've faced that got you to this point and how you persevered and broke through. You have abilities and skills that you picked up along the way. You may not realize them, but they are there. Know that you can tap into that power whenever you want and it is waiting for you to do so if you choose to. The journey from where you are to where you want to go might not be easy. You might fall many times. The question I have for you is, are you able to dust yourself off, refocus and try again?

I hope you say "YES".

SELF WORK: Write an example from your life when you didn't get something the first time and you tried and tried again until you were successful in your endeavor.

5. MEDITATION

"The happiness of your life depends upon the quality of your thoughts."

– Marcus Aurelius

I want to talk about meditation. Meditation has played a major role in my success as a businessman and was my entry into spirituality. It is a very powerful way to gain awareness and self-acceptance. It regulates my moods, relaxes my body and mind, allows me to break through fears and is a calm state I can be active from. By meditating I always can ground myself. And the ability to achieve it is always with me.

About 10 years ago I was very stressed out. My thoughts were spinning really fast and I was getting terrible migraines. When I finally went to a headache specialist the nurse practitioner gave me a magnesium pill, which gave temporary relief. He also suggested that I try meditation. Meditation? I didn't know much about meditation, that was the realm of hippies and spiritualists. But I was in pain and desperate enough to try anything to get rid of the headaches.

The nurse gave me some instructions on how to meditate - focus on and count the breaths. He told me to do it for 20 minutes so I set an alarm. It sounds obvious but it's worth pointing out that we need to breathe to live. No one can breathe for you. By focusing on my breath I was grounding myself to myself. I wasn't trying to ground myself to something or someone outside myself, which are external. My breath is always with me.

Now I want you to pause. Become aware of your breath. Take a deep breath in slowly and let it out slowly. Take another deep breath in slowly and let it out slowly. One more slow deep breath in, pause, now let it out slowly.

After only a month my headaches had gone away. The relief and clarity I got from meditating made me keep doing it. I practiced 20 minutes once a day, sometimes twice if it was a rough day. As I meditated, my mind became less busy with ideas and the stress lessened enough that I noticed the difference. I wasn't as fidgety. I calmed down. I kept on meditating (even now almost 10 years later I still meditate a minimum of 20 minutes a day). Slowly, my stress reduced even more.

The amazing part about meditation is that it gives me a pause to an already busy day. It allows me to relax and refocus, to reboot, to step out of a situation and re-center. That situation is my day-to-day life. In the pause, I can connect with myself and the universe.

I started to notice benefits in my everyday life. I could sit still more easily and focus for longer periods of time. I was able to be more present with people and not stuck in my thoughts. I started to use meditation as a tool in my emotional "toolbox". If I had a lot of work or something that needed total concentration, I would meditate before jumping into the task, getting it done with complete focus, getting it done faster. The amount of work I could successfully handle (what I call my work "basket") became larger and I was more productive. A light-bulb went off in my head and I realized I could change and more than that, that I wanted to change.

Both colleagues and friends commented on how calm and relaxed I had become. I had a "vibe". I was and still am excited to know that's how people see me. It's an added bonus!

Another benefit of meditation for me was I started to learn again. By meditating, my mind went from closed off to being open to new ideas. Like my work basket which had gotten larger, so too my mind had more space for new ideas. I started to read books and attended classes on business, meditation, history and spirituality. This new information allowed me to challenge my old beliefs and how I perceived myself. I no longer had to be stuck in my old beliefs and I started to make a plan on how to become the person I wanted to be.

Now pause again. Become aware of your breath. Take a slow breath in, pause at the top, and slowly let it out. Do this 4 more times and count your breaths. Inhale -1, pause, exhale – 2, inhale – 3, pause, exhale – 4, etc, until you get to a count of 10, then you can start again from 1 or come back to this book. I find it easier when I close my eyes.

The mind is an incredible organism. It is a vast space of infinite potential to make things happen. Anything that can be thought of can be achieved, we just need to give the mind instructions on where to go. We need to program it, to set a course for it to follow so it knows where to go. Wherever we decide to go the mind will follow. That's because the mind is made up of two parts: the conscious mind and the subconscious mind.

The conscious mind is the part that deals with everything you are aware of. It contains everything we are cognizant of at the present moment including thoughts, memories and feelings. This is the creative part of the mind, where ideas come from. We use the conscious mind to think and speak. It is very much in the present moment, reacting to stimuli in the present moment. The conscious mind focuses on what is important to us at that moment.

Your subconscious mind is different. The subconscious is a vault of stories and memories. It's where you hold your beliefs. Its job is to protect you, making sure you do not hurt yourself physically or emotionally. Have you ever waited by a crosswalk and a big truck passes you and you get a little startled? This is your subconscious making you aware of the big truck for your safety and it shocks you to make sure you realize how dangerous it could have been. The subconscious mind also protects us through the ego. The ego keeps us "safe" by using stories and memories to create a narrative about what we can and cannot do. It is through this narrative that we limit ourselves. For example if you lose a lot of arguments or don't get the result you want from doing something, the ego will make you hesitant to engage in or attempt again. The way to change this limiting narrative is through repetition and feelings. By associating an action or a visualization with a feeling, the subconscious will understand that they go together. The more you repeat associating them, the more you imprint a better narrative in the subconscious mind. This is how you will learn to manifest (we will discuss in chapter 9).

Through the practice of meditation we exercise the mind, and just like exercising at the gym, exercising the mind makes it more expansive, elastic, stronger and resilient.

By meditating, I was able to watch what was going on in my mind: what thoughts I had; which beliefs I accepted and where they came from; did they help me or slow me down. I acknowledged that I am responsible for keeping all the beliefs I have, both good and bad. By becoming aware of the beliefs, I could actively change or replace them with new ones that would help me emotionally and spiritually.

I realized that whatever I decided to put into my mind would eventually become reality. The vision I had of myself, who I was meeting, what type of business I was doing and with whom, what types of relationships I had with family and friends, my attitude towards life; these were all things that I put there. So I tried out different beliefs. If a belief did not work, I considered a new one. And through repetition of the new belief it would show itself through me to the outside world, as a profound shift. In the next chapter we will delve into these techniques.

5A.
The Meditation

I chose to infuse the desire to receive money at the beginning of planning this book. I wanted to give you a directional guide. The meditation that you are about to practice will help you visualize and receive money, help you see money in everything you do, and help you see yourself as someone who deserves money. This mindset is powerful.

I suggest you practice this meditation every day. It will reprogram your mind so that you start seeing money everywhere you go. Also, you may tap into something deep that you were unaware was there. If you do, "note" it then come back to the breath.

Before we start this important meditation I want to talk about the act of meditating. I hear all the time from people who have tried meditation, "I'm doing it wrong." So I ask, "what do you mean you are doing it wrong?" They respond "I can't stop the thoughts from coming," and the person feels like a failure.

I want to change the idea in your mind of what a successful meditation looks like, because thoughts will always pop up. I've found that my thoughts have slowed with practice, but they still come up. Whenever I meditate and a thought comes, I "note" the thought and come back to focusing on my breath. The act of trying to meditate is the win, not stopping your thoughts. We are not monks who meditate 16 hours a day. We live busy lives with responsibilities, concerns and tasks that have to be accomplished. So you should feel proud of yourself just for taking the time to meditate.

Read the meditation below. Or have someone read the meditation to you. Read it slowly, pausing after every line. Or you can listen to the audio here : https://www.matthewgw.com/moneymeditation.

Money Meditation:

I would like you to take a comfortable seated position with your back straight. Don't worry too much about some rigid posture, just be comfortable. Place your hands facing up, Ground your feet.

Take a deep breath in and let it out. Close your eyes.
Take a deep breath in your nose, and exhale through your mouth.

Take this next breath, fill your lungs, and let it out.
This next breath I want you to breathe into your belly, into your ribs, into your chest, and then release.

Another deep breath, into your belly, ribs, chest. I want you to hold this one at the top, clench your body as hard as you can. And then just release all of that tension.

Allow your breath to come back to normal.

Become aware of your breath, notice your breath at the tip of your nose or your chest rising and falling.

With your next breath, I want you to appreciate something simple in your life, like that you can breathe, or walk, something you might take for granted. And allow yourself to feel the appreciation in your body.

Now I want you to appreciate something about yourself, something about your body, or your mind. Feel the appreciation in your body. Feel it taking you over. You may feel your mouth even start to curve, as you smile, as the sense of appreciation washes over your entire body.

For this next breath, I want you to appreciate someone in your life. This could be a loved one, a friend, whoever it is. And allow that appreciation to build so much in your body that they can feel it wherever they are, no matter how far away they may be.

Now press your tongue firmly to the roof of your mouth, anchoring this feeling, knowing you can access this whenever you want. And then leave your tongue lightly pressed to the roof of your mouth for the rest of the time.

Imagine yourself outside of a large stadium. Allow that stadium to take shape or size in whatever way you see it. Hear the excitement in the stadium. Feel the excitement.

When you're ready, I want you to go into the stadium. Find yourself in the center of the stadium, the crowd cheering louder than you've ever heard, the ground shaking beneath you, the energy all around you, completely filling your body.

Then you realize that all of these people are cheering for you.

The crowd showers you with money. Your body is a magnet for this money, attracting all of it. Feel it absorbing into your cells. Feel this money filling your body, knowing that you deserve all of it.

These people want you to have their money, you deserve every single bit of it, just for being you. Allow this money to continue to flow towards you, seeing hundreds and hundreds and hundreds of hundred dollar bills, all flowing towards you, and you attracting them like a magnet. You can reach your arms out in your mind, and feel all of this money.

I want you to repeat some phrases in your mind. Say:
I am a money magnet.
Money follows me everywhere I go.
Every breath I take, the more money I make.
Money finds me, everywhere I go.
I deserve all the money people want to give me.
Money is attracted to me, and I am attracted to it.
No matter what I do, more and more money finds me, every single day.
Money flows towards me effortlessly.

Allow that to sink in. Knowing that you're going to be found by money, from now on, everywhere you go.

Now imagine some form of transportation arrives to pick you up. This could be the most beautiful car you've ever seen, a chariot, whatever it is that shows up for you, allow that to show up. Get in this vehicle, and as you leave the stadium, you notice sitting on the seat next to you is a bag full of millions of dollars in cash.

You drive down the street. Everybody showers money at you.

Everywhere you go, money is there, finding you. You accept all of it. Know that money is searching for you and finding you and just sit with that knowledge.

As you're driving along, you see to your right, a treasure chest. You stop and make your way out of the vehicle. Right next to the treasure chest is a key. This key signals to you that this is for you, and that whatever's inside it is meant for you. Open the chest and see what's inside. Allow that to appear, free of judgment, surrendering to whatever is showing up for you.

[longer pause]

Come back to your breath,
feel your feet on the ground,
bring your awareness back to your body,
slowly open your eyes.

STOP.
Do not turn the page until you have completed the meditation.

What did you think of the meditation? Did you like it? Was it empowering? Was it difficult to listen to?

Do an assessment of your reactions during the meditation, specifically the parts about being deserving of and envisioning receiving the money. Were you able to see the money? Were you able to receive it? I hope you were. If you did receive the money, how did that feel? Was it good, uplifting, motivating? Did you feel like you were in the driver's seat?

If it was difficult or you couldn't receive the money, what stopped you? Why did you feel that you couldn't accept it? Did it make you feel gross? Or dirty? Did someone in your past tell you that having money was bad? Or that you aren't supposed to accept money? Why was it hard to receive? Think about it. It's ok if you don't know why. But if you did know, what is it that stopped you from receiving the money?

We all have beliefs around money. Some are good and some do not serve us. Good beliefs include: money gives freedom, money is supportive, I deserve the money I get, I am allowed to earn a good living, I'm allowed to spend my money how I want. Beliefs that do not serve us include: money is dirty, money is the root of all evil, rich people are bad, I will never earn a lot of money, I am not allowed to receive money.

All these beliefs are in our subconscious minds. The beliefs that don't serve us stop us from earning more, taking on new projects, getting a new job, being open to new opportunities, getting a raise, etc. These are limiting beliefs. And it is important to do the "work" on these limiting beliefs, to clear them out and change them into beliefs that are beneficial to you.

There are many ways to change your belief system. Below is one that worked for me. You can also try others (empowering beliefs, Wise Mind, empathy, qualifying statements, Downward Arrow) and see which works best for you. The purpose is to get to the root of the limiting belief and change it to something that is helpful for you. This is the "work" and it brings important change.

I'd like to introduce you to Adam Goodson. He is a master hypnotist who I have worked with. He created "The Limiting Belief Grinder", a series of 26 questions that allows you to focus on a limiting belief then flip it into something that is beneficial to you. Adam has graciously agreed to let me share "The Limiting Belief Grinder" with you.

For the worksheet below, choose a limiting belief to put through the Grinder. Let's say your limiting belief is "I am not allowed to receive money", perhaps someone told you this when you were young. For the first question, "What does this belief limit you from experiencing?" write "it limits me from receiving money" then continue through the rest of the questions. Some of these questions might be tough to answer, but I assure you that you will be able to do it. And on the other side you will be on your way towards change. You should do this for each of your limiting beliefs, for all beliefs from large ones like that one to small beliefs like "I can't make decent coffee"

I have done hundreds of these on many different occasions about different limiting beliefs: about business and money, about family, about friends… anything that was limiting me. When I first got into the work, I was doing 2-3 a day! It felt like a lot and it took focus and patience to get through it. But when I finished, I felt more happy, joyous and free. I still use the "Limiting Belief Grinder" when a limiting belief creeps into my mind.

The Grinder can also be found at the back of the book with more space to answer the questions. You may want to make copies so you can use it whenever needed. It is important that you come back to the "work" frequently, it will allow you to receive the gifts out there in the world.

Limiting Belief Grinder:

What is your limiting belief?

1. What does this belief limit you from experiencing?

2. What emotions are generated by this limiting belief?

3. What emotion(s) would you experience in your life without this limiting belief?

4. If you had not had this limiting belief 5 years ago, how would life currently be different for you?

5. What about 2 years ago?

6. What about 6 months ago?

7. If you conquered this limiting belief today, on a scale from 1 to 10, how significantly would you score the impact?

8. If you lost this limiting belief and could make room for a non-limiting positive belief today as well, how would you score your level of future experiences in 6 months?

9. 2 years from now?

10. 5 years from now?

11. 10 years from now?

12. 20 years from now?

13. Ask your unconscious mind, how have you benefited from this limiting belief?

14. How has this limiting belief been negative for you?

15. How does this limiting belief affect others?

16. In a positive way?

17. In a negative way?

18. If you could flip this belief from limiting to non-limited, from negative to positive, what would it look like when written or typed out?

19. If there was any way to remove this limiting belief from your life, what would that be like for you?

20. If you don't know how to answer the previous question, that is fine. But if you did know, what would it be, what would that look like to you or feel like for you?

21. Since you know you need to now release that negative limiting belief, what is stopping you from that?

22. Could a person or persons help you with releasing this limiting belief? Who and/or what kind of person are they?

23. What would they do to be of service to you as a limiting belief remover?

24. On a scale of 1 to 10, one being the lowest and 10 being the highest, how painful is this belief?

25. When was the first time you felt this way?

26. Do you now know how to overcome this limiting belief?

SELF WORK: Choose a limiting belief and put through the Grinder.

6. LANGUAGE AND GRATITUDE

"Our language is the reflection of ourselves. A language is an exact reflection of the character and growth of its speakers."

– Cesar Chavez

At the end of the last chapter we touched on limiting beliefs, which are the cause of blockages. Releasing blockages is just as important if not more important than visualizing where you are going. When we have a block there is an underlying limiting belief that goes along with that block. That underlying limiting belief makes us believe we are not enough and stop ourselves from getting or achieving what we want. We need to work on breaking those limiting beliefs. If we don't, we won't change. The limiting beliefs are part of the stories we tell ourselves and the language we use to speak to ourselves. Even if we call in things we want, until we clear out the blockages, we will not receive.

Most of us have some negative internal dialogues. These thoughts don't come out but rather sit inside us and are very hard to deal with. The internal voice says you can't do something or you're not enough. And it keeps repeating, making it practically impossible to get off the ride, keeping us frozen in fear. That's why it's so important to deconstruct these underlying limiting beliefs; they keep us from presenting ourselves in the best light. The worst part is the limiting beliefs validate themselves in the world around us, how we perceive ourselves is how we perceive the things around us. So we see examples of the limiting beliefs everywhere.

On the path of enlightenment, becoming enlightened isn't the ultimate achievement, it is the shedding of the things that stop us, which I call "darkness". By shedding the darkness, we lessen the load of limiting beliefs, blockages and negative self-talk so that we can feel lighter by letting go of our baggage.

We are going to work to reprogram the mind to change limiting beliefs into positive beliefs. This will give us more self-esteem and let us feel better about ourselves.

These are examples of the negativity which populate our internal dialogues:

I cannot change

I am not allowed to own a business

I cannot start a business

I cannot learn new skills

I won't make money

I don't deserve money

I'm not allowed to receive money

It will fail

I won't win

There is no use trying

I'm not smart enough

I can't do that

No one cares about me

I'm a loser

What I said was stupid

I'm such an idiot

I'm gonna screw it up

I screwed up again

Only they can have...

I'm not allowed to...

I'm bad at business

I'm not able to make more money

People don't trust me

Clients do not want to work with me

I'm a bad person

What do you tell yourself? Have you ever examined those beliefs that you keep repeating to yourself? Magically, you'll find you've put yourself in situations where everything you've told yourself gets validated. There's a downward spiral of what we say to ourselves being validated in real life which in turn strengthens those negative beliefs. You limit yourself from taking action to be the success we want to be because you're stuck in the negative belief cycle and paralyzed by it.

Where did all this come from? And why do we keep saying it to ourselves? How can we flip the switch?

Carl Jung called this part of ourselves the "ego". Think of it like a program that runs in the subconscious which uses negative beliefs in order to keep us "safe". The ego doesn't want us to get hurt so it tries to maintain the status quo, following the logic that if we don't allow ourselves to take risks and try new things, we can't fail and feel inadequate. These subconscious negative beliefs inadvertently stop us from growing. They are deep beliefs that may have started when we were children and we heard the word "no" from a parent or someone in charge or negative comments or experiences from elsewhere in our lives. They are usually reinforced by our neighborhood or group.

The problem is that while these limit you, they also serve a purpose - keep you "safe". The ego comes into play and stops you from taking that step forward on a new path on which you may or may not fail. The ego sees everything new in your life as a threat that might hurt you so it comes into play to "protect" you, which really means to keep you paralyzed and in place. As a result, you don't take on new challenges or try new jobs, even when they are right in front of you.

Every time you attempt to do something new, something you are not an expert in, the ego jumps in and tells you a negative story about yourself as evidence that you will fail. You say to yourself "I can't do…" Every time you think or speak those words, the belief gets reinforced in the subconscious mind.

I call this the "voice". It's the little voice that says "no you can't" and it shows up in many different forms, for example: "I shouldn't bother because it's raining out so no one is going to want to come into the shop", "no one sees all the hard work I have done", "I'm too tired", "I don't have focus today"… the "voice" goes on and on and slowly we stop ourselves more and more from taking steps that will benefit us.

Sounds pretty bad, right? To get past these beliefs we need to look deep inside to see where these beliefs come from, where they started, and why we still believe these things. By looking at the beliefs we can start to understand how these beliefs keep us "safe." From there we can flip the limiting beliefs and combat the voice so when it shows up we will allow ourselves to try something new without being debilitated by the fear of failure.

There are a number of methods to address negative thoughts. The one discussed in the last chapter is the Limiting Belief Grinder. Here is another method:

Take out a pen and let's shine a light on some issues:
What limiting beliefs do you have about yourself? What do you tell yourself you cannot do? What are your blocks? Start making a list.

Are you scared? Is it hard? Until we start working on the blockages and limiting beliefs, we cannot expect to make great changes in our lives. Change is hard, but it's definitely worth doing. If this is easy, no worries, you'll build up to working on the harder blockages. Remember it's a process, and this process is going to take courage.

If you're having trouble recognizing your negative self-talk, look at the list above to see if any apply to you. Write down at least three and we can start shining light on ourselves. Be honest about what is stopping you, no one else will see this, it's just for you. There is a template at the back of the book.

Once you have a list, ask yourself: why do I believe this to be true, why do I believe that belief about myself? Add these factors to your list.

Take your list and flip the negative beliefs to positive affirmations. "I can't do that" becomes "I can do that". I flipped the list from the beginning of the chapter as additional examples.

I cannot change - I am changing
I am not allowed to own a business - I can own a business
I cannot start a business - I can start a business
I cannot learn new skills - I am learning new skills
I won't make money - I make a lot of money
I don't deserve money - I deserve every penny I get
I'm not allowed to receive money - I am allowed to receive money
I will fail - I am successful
I won't win - I am winning
There is no use trying - I am achieving
I'm not smart enough - I am smart
I can't do that - I can do it
No one cares about me - I am important
I'm a loser - I am a winner
What I said was stupid - I say intelligent things
I'm such an idiot - I am smart
I'm gonna screw it up - I am going to do it correctly
I screwed up again - I am able to fix it
Only they can have that - I can have it

I'm not allowed to... - I am allowed to...
I'm bad at business - I am good at business
I'm not able to make more money - I am making more money
People don't trust me - People trust me
Clients do not want to work with me - clients are excited to work with me
I'm a bad person - I am a good person

Positive affirmations are called mantras. Mantras will help break through limiting beliefs that you've been holding onto. Repeating them will help your mind believe you can accomplish what you want to.

Saying these mantras will help your brain start seeing all the good that you have accomplished. You are instilling them into your subconscious mind and reprogramming the ideas you have about yourself. You can reset your mind to be more optimistic and positive through repetition of positive mantras. You will see yourself differently. You will give yourself a better way of looking at life. You will see yourself as somebody who can succeed, who is allowed to achieve, who can progress, grow... and that's where you need to be. You need to reprogram the negative voice in your head that tells you you can't do something so it will be positive and start giving you permission to do the things that will help you.

Slowly, by repeating these mantras, you will internalize them and start to embody the new you. What you say to yourself becomes your reality. So through repetition of these mantras, your brain will accept them to be true. Whether you think positively or negatively imprints itself in your brain on a scientific level. It's like water dripping onto a soft stone, slowly digging a groove into the stone. That groove can point towards positivity or towards negativity, and your thoughts will follow that groove. The more practice we have thinking positively, the more our brain ingrains positivity and the easier it gets. The more you practice, the easier it will become and in time you will allow yourself to grow to be the person who can accomplish those things you want to accomplish.

SELF WORK: Using the form in the back of the book, write 5 limiting beliefs and flip them to positive affirmations. Say these five mantras ten times each, every day for a week. You can write your own or pick from the list above.

6A.
GRATITUDE

"Cultivate the habit of being grateful for every good thing that comes to you, and to give thanks continuously. And because all things have contributed to your advancement, you should include all things in your gratitude."

– Ralph Waldo Emerson

We often find ourselves looking for outside validation, and compare ourselves to other people. Doing this takes us out of ourselves instead of being internally grounded. We compare and notice what's lacking in our lives rather than what we do have. We feel less than. By comparing what we don't have, we allow an external entity to dictate how we feel. We usually then create a story about why we don't have the things we want. We may blame someone else for what they did to us or say if only I had that thing I would be better. We are constantly looking for outside support and validation in order to maintain our own sense of self. This is a horrible way to live, as the outside is constantly changing and we can always find things that make us feel we are not good enough. Rather than looking outwards, we need to look inwards at what we have. We do this by acknowledging what we have and having gratitude for it. This becomes our constant. We want to start recognizing that what we have is actually really good. In this sense, we can help ourselves by seeing all the good that is happening in our lives on a regular basis.

Gratitude is an attitude.

Gratitude can completely alter your attitude. Being grateful and having gratitude is an incredible way to live and mindset to be in. When we have a grateful mindset we start to notice the little things in our lives that are really good. We start to be content with what is actually going on in our lives and begin to see that things are pretty good. We are able to ground ourselves and appreciate our lives. We can start to see the good in things rather than only seeing what we lack. This contentment will later bring on joy and happiness. We will see ourselves as self-fulfilling ecosystems that allow us to realize the truth, that the state of our lives are really good and that's really important.

Make a list of what you are grateful for. It can be small things, it doesn't have to be something huge. "I'm grateful for..." having breakfast, the warm weather, clean clothes, my children, my husband / wife / partner, my mother / father, the job I have, the snow, listening to my favorite music, my car, my cool shirt... make it about you. What are you grateful for?

Today I'm grateful for:
Working out
Going to the grocery store to buy food so I can eat later
Seeing the sunrise
Taking a shower and having a full breakfast
Going outside for a walk
Chatting with a friend
Meditating
Going to my sister's birthday dinner
Sending out some emails for work
Speaking to a new client
Scheduling my yearly appointment with my doctor

When discussing gratitude, we focus on wins however big or small they may be. We realize all the good and it uplifts our attitude. This is very powerful. I share gratitude lists with friends daily. I write down what I'm grateful for and they respond with their own lists. There are times when I'm in a bad mood or something is not going my way and after sharing or receiving a gratitude list my mood gets better. Writing a list of things that I am grateful for gets me out of my head and into action. Likewise reading a friend's gratitude list makes me focus on their positives and reflect on my own. Taking an action towards good allows me to reprogram my mind away from the negative.

Like with positivity, the more you practice gratitude the more it will ingrain itself in your mind. The dripping water will create new grooves focused on gratitude, making it easier to pay attention to. As you practice recognizing things you are grateful for, you condition yourself to see them more easily and you will start noticing them everywhere, eventually you'll do this without even trying. Having gratitude also forces us to acknowledge things in our lives that are positive, so gratitude also gives us the benefits of positivity.

SELF WORK: Take 5 minutes every day to write a gratitude list. It doesn't have to be long. Start with writing two things, and go from there. Most of my lists are only 5-10 items long. Take out a notebook and write down what you're grateful for. Just by doing this one little task, your outlook for the day will change profoundly and very powerfully.

7.
WHAT IS MONEY?

One's life has value so long as one attributes value to the life of others, by means of love, friendship, indignation and compassion.

– Simone de Beauvoir

Isn't this a book about money? So let's talk about it. What is money?

In its simplest form, money denotes value. We use it to buy goods and services and we pay for that value. And we receive payment for the work we do, which has a value too.

In order to understand money, we need to first define what value is.

The Merriam-Webster dictionary defines it as:

consider (someone or something) to be important or beneficial; have a high opinion of.

Based on that definition we can deduce that if a thing, service or person is useful and beneficial then that thing, service or person has value.

What does value look like? It's a funny question to ask.

Have you ever met someone who is moping around and angry, tired, defeated? Is that representing good value?

The opposite, have you ever met somebody who is really bright and exciting? Positive, confident and optimistic? What is that person like? They give off good energy. You can feel it, right? Is that showing good value?

In my experience, people who do not give a lot of value are also the people who seem to have a shadow over them. They are stuck in their thoughts. They don't listen to their clients. They push away rather than attract. Most of the time I try to stay away from people like that. I limit my time with them because they don't add to my life. Perhaps, they are needy or an energy sucker. These people oftentimes don't attract the type of people they want into their lives. And their income remains lower.

Up till this point we've been doing a lot of work on changing the beliefs that hinder us from shining our light and showing our value. These limiting beliefs and blockages keep us in the darkness and we aren't present. We don't show our best selves when we are stuck. So it is important that we are working on getting rid of those blockages and limiting beliefs that don't help us. We are shedding the darkness to allow in light, give off good energy and become our higher selves.

An analogy I like to use is imagine you are a stained glass window that is very dirty. By working on our limiting beliefs and negative self-talk, we strip layers of dirt from that window and allow more light in.

In the chapters about meditation and about language, we started by looking at what is blocking us from being our best self; until we clear out the blockages, even when we start to attract what we want, we won't be able to receive. Secondly, by changing the negative self-talk and into positive talk we change the way we see ourselves. We start having new beliefs and become grateful for what we have. By doing so we raise our energy, through which we start to present ourselves in a way that shows our value. We start to think more highly of ourselves and do better work, which allows us to present ourselves in our highest forms. People will see the value we bring. We start attracting the clients we want, the most beneficial business partners and the best people to work with. We make ourselves more valuable and people will notice that value.

We're looking at the attributes that allow us to become more valuable. We want to be our fullest person, in essence to become our higher selves. We want to work towards the better version of who we want to be (in the next couple of chapters we will discuss how to get there.) We want to become version 2.0 of ourselves – our higher selves. For some people this may be a fast process, but from experience, it is achieved incrementally, getting better day by day as we do the work and shed the darkness. As we make space for the new, we perform better and become brighter and more open, and that's where the value that we offer shows itself.

If the value we give equates to an amount of money then we must focus on increasing the value we offer. What is that value? How do we raise the value we offer?

This comes down to you and the skill sets you already have, those you will learn, and those you already have but haven't tapped into yet. We each have certain expertise, knowledge or services that we offer, or perhaps we just have a magic touch – that je ne sais quoi. Maybe we know how to do things faster or cheaper, or we offer better quality than the competition, or some nuance makes our service better, or our presentations are superior, etc.

The truth is it has nothing to do with money after all. It's about the total offering of what we are presenting, the way it is presented, and the service level that we give. Payment comes as a result of the value and service.

While this book is about money, it's really about you and what you can bring to the table, that value you offer. The money will come, if the work is good. The money is the reward to our work and the value of our work. We get paid for our work and our service. Our focus is the service that we offer. And it is the quality of service that allows people to get to what they need. When we are in cooperation with our clients, we can help them get what they need. Money is the byproduct of good service. The better the service we offer, which comes from being aligned with our purpose, the more money we make because we are better able to show up for our clients. Customers will see and feel and pay for that value.

Up until now we've been focusing on the inner work of clearing the darkness and creating a good foundation for ourselves and our beliefs in ourselves. In the next chapters we will learn how the universe works, how to work with it and how to start calling in and attracting things we want. We will use the ways the universe works to help us get to where we want to be. My suggestion is that as we start calling in and using the universe to help us manifest what we want, keep working on dismantling the limiting beliefs, saying the mantras, and writing the gratitude lists.

In fact, doing the inner work while working towards your new life gives the best result. I have seen time and time again people who have been working towards their new life for years with no concrete results until they addressed their blockages and limiting beliefs. Once you shift your focus, things start to happen and opportunities start to show up. People in your life will start to see in you things you might not even see yourself. We as the people doing the work don't see our incremental progress. Our friends and family, perceiving us from the outside, will notice our changes faster. People will look at you and see something's changed about you. That's why they'll come towards you. They see your light and are attracted to it and want to see what is going on in your life. They see you in a different way and are attracted to you on both a personal and a business level.

My personal experience is that once I started doing the inner work and shedding the darkness, I got more calls from people. They were checking in on me, seeing how I was doing. I was happy. I was brighter. I had something special about me and people wanted to talk to me. They wanted to tell me what they were up to. They wanted to share their life. They wanted to share their business. I don't know if I was ready for it but the process of growth was happening. So I showed up and accepted the challenge. I said "yes" when people brought projects to me. I was invited to a higher level of work. I could be present and do the work; I was now available.

Negative thoughts and limiting beliefs stop you from being open to the world. Clearing out the negative and the blocks allows you to open yourself up to opportunities. So keep on with the mantras and clearing the limiting beliefs so that you can allow yourself to show your highest value.

Now let's talk about the universe.

SELF WORK: What skills and knowledge do you bring to the table? What value does that offer? What can you do to grow the value you bring?

8.
LAWS OF THE UNIVERSE

*"If I am not for myself,
who will be for me?
And being for myself,
what am I?
And if not now, when?"*

– Hillel

*If you don't like something,
change it. If you can't change it,
change your attitude.*

– Maya Angelou

Think about how big the universe is. It is estimated to be 93 billion light-years in diameter. That means if you were to go the speed of light it would take 93 billion years starting at one side to get to the other side. Wow! Incredible! It is filled with planets and stars, galaxies, blackholes and supernovae, and it is constantly expanding.

The universe echoes back to us the energy and vibrations we put out. We want to put the best energy out there, which is why it is so important to work on our limiting beliefs and blockages so that we can raise our energy level. Another way of saying this is to raise our "vibration" (see below in the law of vibration section).

How we interact and live in the universe is governed by universal laws. These laws help us understand how the universe can support us, and give us pathways to align with it. Until we are shown the laws we may have not realized how our actions and beliefs are affecting us, both for good and bad. Once we understand how our actions and beliefs are mirrored back, we can see what we need to change and make the necessary changes. This awareness allows us to take actions to be more aligned with the universe, and in response the universe starts to support us in our endeavors.

This begs the question, what is needed to do in order to be more

aligned with the universe? The short answer is everything starts with you. You have agency. You have free will. It is your choice to decide how you think and feel. It is your choice to decide whether you do something to change your life or whether you stay put. Regardless of your circumstances, you have the power to change. You have the power to decide how you feel about what is going on in your life. You can decide that today will be a great day and see the world through rose-colored glasses.
Or you can decide to see today as hard and difficult. Both are your choice.

A prime example of this can be found in Viktor Frankl's outstanding book *Man in Search of Meaning*. Viktor Frankl was a Viennese psychiatrist who was a prisoner at the Auschwitz Concentration Camp during the Holocaust, a death camp for mass execution and slave labor. His book gives a detailed account of daily life in the camp: the horrors that occurred, the brutality, the starvation, the mental anguish, the despair, and the hopelessness of his fellow prisoners. What he realized was regardless of circumstances, even being literally in the worst place on earth, a person has the power to choose how he feels about it. He writes, "Everything can be taken from a man but one thing: the last of the human freedoms – to choose one's attitude in any given set of circumstances, to choose one's own way."

What attitude do you want? Do you want to be optimistic? Do you want to see opportunities? To see everything as a chance to learn and grow? To level up? To be able to change your circumstances? Think about the power within you. Think about your courage and perseverance. Tap into your internal strength and know that you can decide the way you would like to think. Later we will see that more importantly, a thought can be a catalyst to take action.

Before we get into action, let us look at the ways which the universe can support us. This will help us understand how to align ourselves with the universe. We'll look at 12 universal laws.

Law of Divine Oneness

Everything and everyone is interconnected. Since everything you do affects everything else, how do you want to live your life? Another way of thinking about this question is, "what do you want written on your tombstone?" Do you want it to read "mean, angry, resentful..." or to say "honest, compassionate, loving, helpful..." It's your choice how you want to interact with the world. Because what you put out there is what you will attract.

A question you might want to ask is: am I being of service? This is important to ask because we want to be supportive and of service to ourselves and to others around us. We want to have the awareness that what we do affects other people. Yes, of course we want money. But the way we go about doing it is important. Are we trying to rob someone? Or are we trying to support and help fulfill a need, making another's life better?

Law of Vibration

Another way to think of the universe is that it is an energy without limits, it is everywhere and is in everything. Energy vibrates. We are energy as well and we vibrate. It is through vibration that we connect with the universe. We are always connected.

Everything has its own unique vibration. Every atom is vibrating at its own wavelength. By working on ourselves, we let go of the darkness we were holding onto that pulls us down. We get to stand tall and go towards the light, higher vibration. We open ourselves to allow the energy of the universe to come to us, flow through us, and emanate from us. It raises our vibrations. We want to have high vibrations, which allow us to attract better things into our lives.

What is a high vibration? A high vibration is great energy. It's openness to ideas, people and things. It is allowing ourselves to see new opportunities, it is being available to oneself and others. It is being present. It is connection. It is beauty. It is going towards the light. It is positivity. It is joy.

What is low vibration? Low vibration is being closed to the world. It is living in fear, resentment, and anger. It is feeling like a victim. It is shutting ourselves off from other people and ourselves. It is being stuck in negative thoughts. It is being closed off to receiving from the universe. It is a dark cloud.

By raising our vibration, we open ourselves up to the world. We become a channel of our higher purpose and allow the light of the universe to flow through us. We can feel openness, are energized and are excited by life and the opportunities that present themselves to us. The more work we do to eliminate negative thoughts and clear blockages, the higher our vibrations ascend. We attract and receive gifts at the vibrations we are at.

Money has a vibration too. Every amount of money has a certain vibration. In order to receive a certain amount of money, we need to be on the vibration level of the money we want to receive.

Have you ever received $100? Have you ever received $1,000? $10,000? $20,000? $50,000? $100,000? Why did you receive that money? It's because your vibration matched the vibration of that amount of money. By raising ourselves to the vibration, we align ourselves to receive that amount of money.

Law of Attraction

The Law of Attraction is probably the most well-known law. It states that what you think and what you feel is what you will attract into your life. You attract the vibration you are on. Essentially, you attract the things that are where your vibration is at. It's the concept of like attracts like. If you want better things to come into your life you need to be at their vibrations to attract them. You need to already be there to draw the higher-vibration people and opportunities into your life.

If we come from a place of positivity, service, happiness, compassion and love, the things we will receive will match those qualities. When we clear out the blockages and work on our limiting beliefs, we raise our vibrations and open ourselves to attract the gifts of those higher vibrations. These gifts come in the form of opportunities, good business associates, new ideas and money.

Law of Transmutation of Energy

Everything is in constant motion and is changing. This is important to us because that means by working on ourselves, even in the smallest way, our energy and our vibration will change. Even in difficult mindsets we can choose to improve our thoughts and raise our vibration. We are not stuck. We have the power to change ourselves and our circumstances, and since everything is interconnected everything around us changes as well.

The same is true with taking action. When we take action towards the lives we want, opportunities around us will start to shift in the direction of our actions. This is also true in the opposite direction. When we spend time with people who are heavy or difficult, or we start doing things not in our best interest, our vibration will drop and affect our surroundings as well.

Law of Correspondence

I like to call this law "language part 2". It states that any ideas/thoughts/beliefs you have about yourself are what you project and they dictate how you see the world. We all want to be able to look at ourselves in a good light and see that our lives are good. This is why being grateful is so important. When we're grateful, we put gratitude into the world and announce that things are good.

In the last chapter we looked at the language we use about ourselves and established that it's important we talk about ourselves in a positive rather than a negative light. There's a small detail in here that's very important for us to take note of.

The universe can only echo back what you put out there, so precisely what you say is important. When you say "I need something" (car, house, money...) what is the universe actually hearing? It's hearing "I need..." not the thing you want. So what is the universe going to give back to you? Remember this is an echo chamber, it's going to give you more "need". Whereas to actually get those things, you have to already "have" them so we use the term "I have" and "I am". Because if you "have" something the universe is going to give you more of it. If you want money, say "I have money." If you want a job, say "I have a job." If you want new opportunities, say "I have opportunities." The universe will mirror it back to you. It will give you what you put out there. This is why the mantras in the last chapter are in the present form. The universe will acknowledge that you "have" these and give you more of them.

Law of Inspired Action

The Law of Inspired Action is connected to the Law of Attraction. We must take action to show the universe that we mean business and allow what we are manifesting to come into our lives.

When you are aligned with your truth you will be inspired to take action towards your purpose. This alignment will be the catalyst to inspire you to do what you have to do. It will make you focused and determined.

There are two important aspects here: (1) Think about your purpose; you might want to ask yourself: What is important to me? What do I want to be doing? (2) Then take action. Take the first step towards that purpose. When we are truly aligned with ourselves nothing can stop us from working towards and completing our purpose. By being aligned with your purpose, you will be inspired to take action.

After this chapter the book is dedicated to pursuing your ideal new life and taking action towards it.

Law of Cause and Effect

Every action produces a reaction. If you create something that is valuable to society you will also receive something that's valuable to you. If we create, we will receive. It can be in the form of money, opportunities, introductions, partnerships, etc. Keep taking actions to bring more opportunities for you to receive.

This works similarly for your attitude. If you have good thoughts, are compassionate and come from a place of gratitude, all that goodness will come back to you. The opposite is also true, if you are negative, lie or cheat, these will come back to you as well. Understand that the reaction may not come right away.

Law of Compensation

Similar to the law of Cause and Effect, this law states that whatever you put out in the world you will be compensated for. It's important when you create your business that you realize that you will get compensated for that work that you put in. You will be paid in direct value of that work. We receive payment that is equal to the value we create so we want to provide the best value possible.

Law of Gender

Energies fall into two categories: masculine energy and feminine energy. Each one of us has both masculine and feminine energy within us, regardless if we are male or female. We need both energies to be successful and use them for different purposes. Masculine energy is defined by creating, organizing and taking action. Feminine energy is empathetic, compassionate and receives. We use both of the energies when creating a business or going after a job or a promotion. The masculine energy gets us into action and we create. Then, we need to use our feminine energy to allow us to receive and to connect.

Law of Relativity

The Law of Relativity tells us that everything is neutral. As humans we like to label things as good or bad, better or worse, more or less than. We like to compare things. We do this because it allows us to categorize. We label things from our perspective from the information we gather. This can be a problem as we label from perspectives which are impacted by our experiences and what we've been told rather than a neutral perspective. We may label something as "bad" because we are comparing when in fact everything is just fine.

In fact everything just "is".

This is why having a gratitude practice is so important. By being grateful for what we have and the successes we are making, regardless how small, we stay above the trap that keeps us in the space of "it cannot be done" or "I am not good enough" which can happen when we compare ourselves to others.

Law of Rhythm

The Law of Rhythm states that everything has a cycle and nothing stays in one state forever.

In our everyday lives, we have good days and we have bad days. Things are constantly changing, in us and around us. Often we get stuck in a place of negativity and it may feel like we are there forever, only to have the next day be the best day. Everything goes up and down in a cyclical fashion. We may try something new and not be good at it, only to find out a month later we are excellent at it. Or we may get out of alignment and think it's all over, but after a moment of rest and perspective of what is going on, we get our groove back.

In short, nothing is static. Everything changes, including the things that are troubling you right now.

Law of Polarity

The Law of Polarity states that there are two sides to everything. Everything has an opposite: up and down, bad and good, darkness and light. This should bring comfort as it means our current circumstances can be changed.

When we first start out on the journey of self growth and awareness we may find ourselves in a dark place, a place we don't want to live in. What we want to achieve is the opposite, to go towards the light, a good place, a place of happiness and joy.

If we have a scarcity mentality where we worry there's never enough, know that if we do the work, both internally and for our businesses, we can get to a place of abundance.

SELF WORK: What does support mean to you? How can you support yourself?

9.
MANIFESTATION

"What you think, you become.
What you feel, you attract.
What you imagine, you create."

– Buddha

We need to give the Universe direction in order for it to help us get to where we want to go. By giving direction, the Universe knows you mean business and you have a plan. Create the image of who you want to be, and call this new vision into your life. This process is called Manifestation. We need to manifest this ideal new life.

Think about what you want to bring into your ideal new life. Is it a new job? A promotion? To start your own business? To grow your business? Or is your goal to grow into your higher self?

This is the fun part! First, visualize the life you want. Do this by creating a picture in your mind of the life you would like to have. It can be a vague image at first, but it is better to get all the way down into the little details. You want to see yourself in that space. Have fun with this process, allow your mind to run. There is no limit where you can go. If you can see that new life, it is only a matter of time until it will come to fruition.

The second part of manifestation is to experience the feelings you will feel when you are in that new life. Actually feel them. Allow the feelings associated with the new life to overcome you. Embody them. Know what it feels like to be accomplished and strong. Money in the bank. People needing you and your services. When you do this work, you are sending a message to the universe about your desired life. What you want to accomplish, and where you see yourself. The universe will echo back what you put out there.

Let's get into the process of manifesting. Take out your notebook and pen or use your phone.

Like the mantras, make sure you write your visualization in the present form. Here are some examples: "I have a thriving business", "I am the owner of a company", "I am getting promoted", etc.

Here are a number of prompts to help you visualize the new vision of yourself:

What does your life look like in that new space?
What work do you do?
Where are you working?
Are you the owner?
Did you get a promotion?
Did you get a new job?
Where do you live?
What does your house or apartment look like?
How do you look physically?
What are you wearing?
How do you hold yourself?
How do you act?
How do you behave?
Who are your clients?
What are your interactions like with your clients?
How did you step up in your work?
What type of car do you drive?
What color is it?
What does the car feel like?
How does it sound and smell?
How much money are you earning?
What does it feel like to have that money in your bank account?
Where do you go to eat?

What do you order?

What does it feel like to pay for that meal?

Where do you go on vacation?

What type of hotel do you stay in?

How does it feel waking up in that room?

Below are some prompts to help you focus on feelings of this new life. As the feelings come up, embody those feelings. Become the feelings. This is what it is going to feel like in your new life. Know that this is who you are. And you have always had it in you.

How does it feel to be winning?

How does it feel to be confident?

How does it feel to be the person you are describing? Good? Exciting? Strong?

Are you happy?

Are you calm and relaxed?

Do you feel good?

This new life that you have visualized has a vibration. And by manifesting, visualizing and feeling, you raise your vibration to the level of this new life. You align to the universe at this new vibration and the universe echoes back to you "gifts" - all the things that will help you and support you to have this life at this higher vibration.

The important thing about this process is to keep visualizing this truth in your mind. The life you want to create. That life will start to be imprinted in your subconscious mind. Do it for 5-10 minutes a day.

To solidify this, write down your visualized ideal life in the present tense. And by putting it in writing you are solidifying that idea. Take 10 minutes a day and write. Focus on this new image of yourself. Feel it. Know that it is true.

The Universe will help you. Through visualization we allow the Law of vibration to start to take hold. You will attract the type of people you want, the type of business you want, and the relationships that will propel you forward. You will become a magnet to them. The life you are manifesting will become your reality.

SELF WORK: Write out what your visualized ideal new life looks like and what you look like in this new life. Remember to put it in the present tense.

10.
PLAN

Action is the foundational key
to all success.

– Pablo Picasso

We know where we are, and using the visualization of our new life and the business or type of job we want in the future, we see the endpoint of where we want to be and in between is the process. We want to lay out our process and develop action steps to guide us to the life we want to have. These action steps will direct us in the process of creation.

It is very important to create a plan. The plan gives guidance on next steps to take. The plan can change and we will discuss that in the chapter about change, but as a starting block you will have more focus and direction by writing down all the details you have to accomplish. I like to think of it as a checklist. Things that I can do and check off to move me closer to success.

Until you have a plan, it is just a wish. When you have a plan, there is a track to stay on. Think of yourself as a business and this business has its most important work ahead. How do we make sure that we stay on track? We need a plan. We set our intentions with a plan and write them down so our intentions are emblazoned on the paper. We have already written down our new life and now we will work towards that new vision. Let's look at this new vision and see what we need to do to get there. This list should include all the little details that make up this master project.

This next part is very important. I am going to ask a lot of questions to get you to think about all of the little parts and details that are needed to make sure you are set up to succeed. The more details the better, but if you do not have an answer that is ok too. You can always come back to them. These questions are to get you thinking and set you up for success.

Let's discuss what it'd look like if your goal is in business. First we'll look at starting or growing your company. Then we will look at getting a promotion or a new job.

1. What are you selling? Is it a product or a service?
2. What is that product or service? What are the offerings? If you have a few options, what are they? Why do people need your product/service?

If it's a product, where are you getting it? Do you have a design? If it's a service, how are you going to do it? Answer in detail.

3. Do you have a logo? What are the colors of the logo? How does it look?

4. Do you have a website? How many pages do you need on your website? (I find a 3 page website is pretty good to start with – an about us, offerings page, and contact page.) About us – how did this company come into being? Why do you exist? Offerings – use what you wrote above in #2.

5. Who is your target client? Give a full description of who they are and why they need your product/service.

6. How will you reach your clients? Where can you advertise your product/service? What do you need to say in your advertisement to get people to reach out and purchase the product/service? What is your message?

Maybe you're working on getting a promotion or getting a new job.

1. What is the new job or promotion you want?

2. What skill sets do you need for the job and do you have them? If not, where can you learn those skills? Is there a school or online?

3. What steps are needed to get to that space so you can get that job? Answer both mental and physical steps.

4. Who do you need to talk to? Maybe you need to talk to someone in the company about what you need to be qualified. Maybe you have a friend who works in the industry and can give advice. Or you met someone at an event. They might have a job for you or give you information to help you to get that job.

5. These questions are all very very important to make sure you're getting noticed. What additional effort do you have to put in? Is there a way to stand out from everyone else?

6. Do you need to leave your company for a new one to get a promotion?

Let me give you an example. When I was first asked to write this book I didn't know what to write about. So I made a plan of all the topics I wanted to cover. All of the ideas about business and spiritual practices that I knew would be beneficial for me to share. As I had more awareness of what I was doing and what I needed to write, as the project became more robust, I updated the plan adding new topics and ideas I wanted to discuss and developed the topics and ideas. One by one I checked off the topics and ideas I needed to write about.

Also, by having a checklist you see what you are actually doing, not what you think you are doing. You can see what tasks need to be done; what you have accomplished; and what you still need to work on. Awareness is key here. When we keep track of what we're doing, we see what we're missing and where we can improve.

I am asking you to get into all the details because for the majority of you at some point you are going to get stuck. The "voice" is going to come into play and tell you that you aren't good enough and you cannot succeed, and you are going to lose faith in that big picture of your new life and what you are trying to accomplish. By breaking it down to smaller steps, it becomes easier to finish the different aspects of your project. There is a saying that if you are going to eat an elephant, best to do it one bite at a time. It's no longer this large daunting project, rather smaller bits each culminating in the whole. One task at a time.

The "voice" is a killer. It destroys motivation and makes you feel bad so that you do not want to push forward. It's your ego saying what you are doing is not very good. So it's going to try to stop you, to make every excuse possible so you don't go ahead and do the work that you need to do to create your new life. This is an issue because the "voice" is going to keep telling you can't finish this project and this is the reason why it's so important, especially in the beginning to clear out your limiting beliefs.

The "voice" hides in the limiting beliefs and blockages and uses them to demotivate you.

So how do you fight through the negativity of the "voice", the thing that's going to stop you from making progress? In order to combat the "voice" you need to have continued momentum. You do this by creating action steps that allow you to maintain work at a certain level of quality. This is why writing out your plan is so important. It is a guide to what actions your need to take in order to get your business running or to go towards a promotion.

In the next chapter we will discuss how to maintain continued momentum. But it really starts out with having a set of action steps. Your plan will allow you to stay focused on the important tasks that will allow success.

SELF WORK: Create your plan. As a reference, you can use the questions I listed above. Be as detailed and specific as possible to help you really visualize your action steps.

11.
MINIMUMS

*"If I can offer you some advice...
just start small and that's how
you really change your life.
You incorporate small changes
one by one into your daily routine.
Then all of the sudden
it's the routine that's driving you.
And it just becomes your life."*

– Greg Young

I want to share with you a method of motivating yourself in a way that will help you grow. This is a really powerful method that will not only help you build your business or yourself, it will propel you as you grow. It will give you a baseline for where you are and will push you forward with incremental growth. In a simple sense, you start small and build on your abilities so you gain confidence as you grow.

In chapter 9, when we discussed how to manifest, we talked about the big picture items: where you see yourself in the future and what you ideally want to accomplish. It's really important to do that exercise as it will help you manifest and raise your vibration. In chapter 10, when we made a plan of action, we wrote out all the different aspects that go into our company or towards getting a job or promotion.

The concept I'm about to share with you is about your everyday activities, the things you need to do to run your business or get promoted. The action steps needed to reveal what you are manifesting. The way this exercise is set up will push you to want to do more work. It's about taking action which the universe will see and will help to bring about what you are manifesting.

Before I get to the concept I want to talk about the way people are taught to motivate themselves. People like to use the word "goal". While the word seems pretty simple, Merriam-Webster dictionary defines it as "the end towards [which] effort is directed". The issue with this word, "goal" is all the things we attach to it. Sometimes we set really high goals, like to make

$1,000,000 this year even though last year we only earned $50,000. While this is a worthwhile "goal", there is a major issue that comes up if we don't achieve our goal.

It's like the phrase "shoot for the stars: if you don't hit it you will at least land on the moon." We work really hard towards that "goal". We often are spinning our wheels thinking we're getting closer to that "goal"; we work crazy hours, yet after 6 months we realize we haven't gotten anywhere close. We look back at all the work we did and try to analyze what we did wrong. Even if we did well we still didn't hit our goals. This takes up a lot of energy and time, because by setting targets that are out of reach, we set ourselves up to fail.

When we try something and fall short, we feel bad. Maybe we get discouraged. Maybe we don't want to try again. Maybe we quit altogether.

Think about this common occurrence:

Have you ever made new year's resolutions?
Did you keep those new year's resolutions?
If you did, how did that feel?
If you didn't, how did that make you feel?

The problem is that when you say you're going to do

something and then don't, you feel bad. You feel like a loser, an underachiever, somebody who can't accomplish what they wanted to get done. And often when we're starting a new venture or trying to make headway in our career, when we start feeling like we're not doing well, we lose confidence and slowly give up.

That is no way to live.

I'm going to try to get you to form a habit of achieving by getting and maintaining momentum. I want you to feel like a winner. I want you to feel good about yourself for the work that you're doing and to make progress.

Let me ask another question. How do you feel when you say you're gonna do something and then actually you do it?

It feels better when you do accomplish what you set out to do.

Between feeling bad and feeling good, which is better? Which serves you more?

If you say you're going to do something but don't, you feel miserable, depressed, like a loser, an underachiever, a slacker. In contrast, when you set a bar and are able to jump over it, that feels good.

We can teach ourselves to achieve, we can form habits of success by setting MINIMUMS in our life, whether in business or otherwise. Minimums are the low bars we know we will accomplish. They make us feel good and build our confidence. Then we can raise the bar a little when we're ready to. Reach that first minimum, feel good, have that sense of achievement, and raise the bar again. This feeling is addicting. Saying you're going to do something and achieving it releases endorphins, which make you feel good.

One of the problems in business is we congratulate and pat ourselves on the back only when we make a big sale or meet a goal. Yes, sales are important, but there are also so many smaller tasks that need to get done in order to make that sale. When we only allow ourselves to feel accomplished when we make a sale, we are setting ourselves up for disappointment. We don't make many sales in the beginning because we are learning, building ourselves and our skill sets. We are learning all the things that need to occur for that sale to happen. All the small tasks of developing a product or a service, creating content and marketing material, putting up advertisements, and client outreach and follow up. By putting all the pressure on making a sale to feel good, we discount all the other work we've done. If we don't make sales we are demotivated and feel negative.

Here are a couple of examples of how minimums work:

Let's say you want to bench press 300 lbs. If you try to do that right away, you will not be able to and will hurt yourself badly. Start with a number you know you can do. Let's say 25 lbs. It's a bit of a struggle in the beginning, but eventually you can lift 25 lbs easily and you feel good about the result. Add some more weight. Now you are lifting 35 lbs. Feel good about your accomplishment. And when that becomes easy to do, add more weight. Eventually you will get to 300 lbs.

Now a work example: you want to promote your brand. In order to get eyes on your product or service you need to post on social media. You may not be very good at posting yet. You are new to this and it's nerve racking because you want the posts to be perfect. The perfect tone, the perfect content, the perfect phrasing… You've heard to have success you need to post 3-5 times a day. You start on the first post and keep editing and rewriting for 2 hours! Again, you are new at this. You publish the post then realize it'll take forever to write the other three posts and you won't have time to do everything else you need to do to run the business. You feel discouraged. Maybe you stomp your feet. You tell yourself this can never get done. And I don't know about you but I find this situation very deflating and demoralizing, so it's hard to continue.

Let's flip the script using the concept of minimums: With the minimums you tell yourself you're going to publish one post every single day. While it still takes you 2 hours to write each post you are able to publish one every single day. Once you post, you are done posting for the day and can work on other things. You feel good that you finished the post, finished that assignment. Over time you will get better and the post that used to take 2 hours becomes easier because you are doing it every day – one a day. Practice makes perfect. And that post now only takes you thirty minutes to write. You decide to raise the bar a little now to two posts a day. As you get even better at writing posts, it takes you only 20 minutes. Your ability to write posts has gotten a lot better. Again, raise the bar a little, this time to three posts a day. Only ever raise the bar to something you can accomplish. In no time you are writing posts easily and soon have no problem writing five posts a day.

The point is, set the bar to something you know you can achieve until that becomes easy. Then raise the bar to a new level you know you can now accomplish. Succeed in the task, get better, feel good about yourself. You will not get overwhelmed. And step by step, you accomplish more of what you want to get done.

When you start your venture, solicit customers, go for a job, or set yourself up for a promotion I hope you get it on the first try. I really do. For those with of the right luck and skill, hats off to you. For the rest of us who need to build momentum, minimums is a way of getting things moving.

Minimums make you feel powerful, like a winner. Minimums allow you to realize you can be successful. Because you set achievable bars for your tasks, you get them done, you feel good and then you're done for the day. You've accomplished everything you said you were going to do that day. Give yourself a gold star. And imagine if you keep going and accomplish more after you finish your minimums. How would that feel? You're gonna feel pretty good about yourself. It's a bonus to whatever you decided you were getting done that day. You will gain confidence in your skillset and start feeling good about yourself because you did everything you said you would.

Do you see how this can help you propel yourself in business? Do you see how doing what you set out to do will make you feel good?

I want you to feel good about yourself. I want you to feel like you're doing the right things and going in the right direction. Not that you feel overwhelmed. Not that you feel like you're going to mess up. Not that you feel like a loser because you haven't accomplished everything you wanted to. You see with self development and also with business, there are things you have to get done. You don't want to get stuck under a pile of papers and allow them to build up. Or to feel like there's not enough time in the day to get everything done.

By creating minimums and achieving them we are teaching ourselves how to win. We are programming ourselves to accomplish things so we can feel capable in the work we are doing. When we set goals that are out of reach, we condition ourselves to fall short, to fail and to feel bad. However, when we implement minimums we allow ourselves to see, through experience, that what we wish to accomplish is possible. And it motivates us to do more.

Like the weightlifting, you set your minimum to something you can accomplish. When completing it becomes easy, you raise the bar a little. That is how you grow.

Let me say this a different way. Do something and get good at it. When it becomes easy, add more tasks. Make sure the tasks are things we can achieve so we accomplish what we set out to do.

Your learning curve may be faster or slower, but either way by accomplishing what you want to get done, you feel better about yourself. When you see results you want to continue, building momentum. You keep doing the things that will help you become a success, the necessary tasks that build your business. Endorphins kick in. You pat yourself on the back as you know you are doing a good job. And instead of beating yourself up for not finishing all the work, you create little wins which will propel you to accomplish what is needed.

In a matter of months you are adding more and more to your daily to-do list, and getting it all done! You accomplish your minimums, feel good, raise the bar a little and keep going. You feel like a winner. This helps get you into a state of flow where you're able to accomplish everything you set out to do. You are the one who drives the business, rather than the business pushing you around. You are not in a constant game of catch up; you are in control, pushing your business forward.

This method can be used in lots of different scenarios in your life.

Is there something you like to do? Play an instrument? Learn a new language? Work out?

How does it feel when you're learning another language and suddenly realize you're using the correct grammar and pronunciation? When your vocabulary grows, how does that make you feel?

If you're a runner, how does it feel that when you started out you could barely run a mile and now you're contemplating a half-marathon?

How does it feel when you make progress? Does it make you feel good? I'm sure it does. All of us want to achieve, it is ingrained in our being.

We want to feel accomplished, and minimums help make that happen. All of us want to be successful in what we do, to feel good about it and to feel pride in our achievements.

But we often don't set ourselves up to succeed. When you try to do too much and you fail, how does that feel?

Think about playing an instrument. Maybe you buy a guitar and think to yourself, "Yeah, man, in two weeks, I'm going to be like Eric Clapton or Keith Richards." We all know that's not happening. You have to learn to play chords first. Then to play scales. Then play a very simple song, and you'll be ecstatic! Over time you get better and stronger. And you learn more and more so eventually you can play complicated songs easily.

That is the power of minimums.

SELF WORK: Go back to what you wrote in chapter 10 that you need to do for your business. Now write minimums for those tasks.

12. PERFECTION

"Have no fear of perfection – you'll never reach it."

-Salvador Dali

I want to share an idea that has helped me throughout my business and personal growth process. One of my biggest problems is perfection. I want it done right. So much so that I would paralyze myself from getting anything done if it wasn't going to be perfect. I'd dream up big plans, write them down, start working then bam, I was stuck. Paralyzed by the voice and blockages. Comparing myself to others who were more established. Thinking I would never succeed.

I remember the first time I sent an email promoting my business to all my clients and friends. I wrote it. It looked pretty good. All I had to do was press send. The voice came in. "How will I be perceived?" "Will they like me?" "Will they be impressed?" "Is it good enough?" I froze. I was scared. My mind was freaking out because I knew I had to press send. I stared at the email draft, drank 10 cups of coffee and distracted myself by running around the office 30 times. I must have looked like a crazy person from anyone looking in the office window.

Then I remembered some advice Greg had given me:

"There is no perfect, only done."

What simple advice! I thought about what Greg had said and pressed send. I could have stared at my computer for hours and never felt it was good enough. It's better to send a good-enough email than to obsess over it for days and never hit send.

In the end, people responded by congratulating me. Wanting to help me out. Some people called on my services, and I was off to the races.

There was so much fear about even starting. Am I allowed? Am I deserving? It all came down to the same internal thought "I am not enough". Whether it's starting a business, going after a job or promotion or doing work on yourself, the important thing is to take that first step forward. For me it was to give myself leeway that I could mess up and be ok with it.
Being able to start small is important. You don't have to be the

best on day one, "Rome wasn't built in a day." On this journey of self-growth to create wealth and money in your life, there are things you'll need to address when they pop up. In the beginning of my journey, everything I did was a challenge and felt difficult. I was so afraid of messing up. Mind you, a lot of what I was doing was by myself. So I was the one criticizing my own actions. Insane really.

I took one tiny step forward, did something I knew I could accomplish and got confident. Then I added another thing. Eventually, I had a slew of things I was doing every day. Both my spiritual program and my business work started to get bigger, adding new things to help me grow. I was changing and what I needed for my growth needed to change as well.

Like the meditation we did in chapter 5, the important element is that you take action. Everything you do to clear out the blockages so that you can receive money is action. So is everything you do towards the creation of that money. Once you take action you will find the support you need to rise up to meet you. So take action. Go forward.

SELF WORK: Write something you want to do but haven't because you're afraid you'll never do it quite right. What are those fears? Remember that fears are limiting beliefs. Now use the Limiting Belief Grinder to flip them.

13.
CHANGE

"The world as we have created it is a process of our thinking. It cannot be changed without changing our thinking."

- Albert Einstein

We are doing the work, clearing out limiting beliefs and blockages, manifesting our new realities, writing our plans and started working on them. What could happen? Change! The only constant in the world is change. So get ready for it. Starting on the path of self-growth is starting on the path of change. That's what we're working for. We change as we grow. New things, new challenges and new opportunities are going to come and we'll need to utilize new-found tools to handle them. We'll need to deal with this change. And the way to do that is to adapt.

The first thing is to have awareness that there will be change. We can expect things to change and welcome the changes and opportunities that come with it. We can prepare for change and be ready for it when it comes. However, many people want things to stay in an orderly fashion, and when something changes they are not ready for it. They get frustrated.

As we grow as individuals, we learn about ourselves and what we need in order to have peace of mind and success. We start realizing what types of support we need, who we want to spend our time with and what things are good for us. These may be completely different than what we have now. We learn about our capabilities and how far we can push ourselves, as well as our skill sets. We find new tools we will have to learn to aid ourselves in our growth. We will need to keep learning new skillsets as we grow. Things that gave us comfort before may not do so later in our growth. We may need new mantras or different strategies to continue to grow.

I know from my own experience that a lot of the skillsets I was focusing on early in my journey are now second nature to me. The tools I need to keep growing are very different from what I needed at the beginning. My journey has had highs and lows and what I needed changed often.

Through my journey, I have learned a lot about what I need to give myself support and to grow. I have learned which types of things push me up and allow me to raise my vibration. This gives me an opportunity to try things on my own personal journey, to look at new ideas and to find what interests me.

Trial and error is a very important aspect of business and of spiritual growth. While we want things to come organically, we also want to force change in order for us to have faster progress in our spiritual and business growth. For this we use the scientific method.

The scientific method tells us to (1) determine what we want to test, (2) ask a question or propose a hypothesis, (3) test our hypothesis, (4) observe the results, to (5) determine the answer to our question or hypothesis.

We can ask ourselves, what would happen if we tried "this"? "This" being whatever we want to try. We develop a plan then try it out. Afterwards we look at the results. We may or may not have been right with our hypothesis that doing "this" will produce a certain result. It may be a different result than we were expecting, but it nonetheless gives us new insights and understandings. This system is called the scientific method and it is a very powerful tool because it gives us the ability to question and test new ideas and thoughts.

The scientific method applies to both our spiritual and our business growth. We test new theories, ideas and practices in our spiritual life. We try new marketing and business strategies to grow our businesses or get us closer to a promotion or new job. There is nothing wrong with trying something to see how it will work out. It will give you knowledge and perspective as well as add to the toolbox we will need to succeed in our endeavors. See what works and what doesn't. Take notes and track the results.

The act of tracking what we are doing will improve our results. Tracking makes us aware of what we are actually doing, not what we think we are doing. Tracking is a very powerful tool. We can see the actual results of our actions rather than thinking we are doing something we are not.

One example: for my spiritual growth I was saying mantras and journalling every day. This helped me stay focused. I knew from analyzing my writing that I had blocks and limiting beliefs that I needed to overcome. I realized I had to do more digging into my past to get over them. I tried a number of different methods and eventually landed on the "Limiting Belief Grinder" as the method that worked best for me.

Another example: part of my business involves writing advertisements for new homes I brought to market. I'd write one way, then change one thing and see how potential clients responded to it. Why one thing? Because I wanted to see if that specific change brought me more clients and what types of clients reached out to me. By keeping track of the changes I was able to see what worked and what didn't. Over time I integrated the successful practices into my advertisements. The way I write advertisements now always gets top quality clients who are ready to buy.

Not everything we try will work, be ready for that too. But the important thing is to take that step forward. Try everything and take notes. When we try something, we usually learn something new. Perhaps we've learned that something doesn't work, that gives us perspective. We tweak it and try again. We keep trying new and different ideas. This by itself will make us more flexible allowing us to adapt to our ever-changing environments. By training ourselves to be ready for change, we adjust much faster.

We learn from our wins and we learn from our misses, both are important. Some of my best learning moments were when I tried something and nothing happened. See what works and what doesn't. Allow for change to occur, allow yourself to grow.

SELF WORK : Write why you resist change.

14.
AFTER-THOUGHT

*"And the day came
when the risk to remain tight
in a bud was more painful than
the risk it took to blossom."*

- Anais Nin

When I reflect on the process of my growth in becoming the businessman I am today, there is a lot that comes to mind. This process is ongoing. I am constantly working on and developing myself to get better and become my higher self. I use the tools and ideas shared in this book on a regular basis. Now, my work basket is quite large, the types of projects are bigger and more interesting than even a few years ago. I have more confidence in myself and my abilities. Every year I am more grounded in myself and stronger. My focus is on the practices that help me grow as a person and grow my business.

My ability to achieve success didn't happen in one day. It took time, patience, tenacity and perseverance. It was important for me to focus on my ultimate achievement, I used meditation to ground myself and ignore all the outside noise so that I could focus. In the calm and quiet of meditation, I'm able to look into my beliefs, understand what is limiting and blocking me and work through them so that I can move forward with confidence and certainty.

I became aware that I am not alone and am supported by the universe which is pushing me forward. I learned that the universe would support me only if I took action towards my ideal life. I took an inventory of my abilities and realized that while money is what I am working towards, the way to receive that money is by using my abilities to provide a service and give value. Through developing and mastering these abilities I could offer more value and be rewarded for the value I offered.

It was important for me to realize that I was responsible for myself and my outlook. I was ultimately responsible for my achievement and the life I wanted to have. It was up to me to make that happen.

The next step was to create the life I wanted. By using manifestation, I visualized what my ideal life looked like. I saw my work, the type of clients, the type of success and me receiving the reward for my services all the while allowing myself to feel what it would be like in that life. This action gave the Universe the direction of what I wanted to achieve. "Wishing" and "doing" are two very different things and the universe only supports those who are doing and in action, which is why it was important for me to draw up a plan. A plan gave me guidance and outlined all the work that I would need to accomplish for my business. All of the tasks that I needed to do in order to get my company up and running or get my promotion.

From here, I acted on those tasks that were needed and motivated myself by giving myself work that I knew I could accomplish, minimums, setting low bars so that I could jump over, giving myself high fives and feeling good. I realized that it was through repetition of these tasks that I would gain expertise and that the tasks would become easier such that I could do more as time went on. I understood that I would not do them perfectly the first time. Instead, "good-enough" was a good place to start, knowing that my work would get better over time the more I did it.

Lastly, I accepted that change is an inevitable part of my work, whether market conditions changed from what I expected or continued improvement needed me to redirect my work. I also realized that I could use change to push me to learn new skills that would be beneficial to my work and my life. I understood that the changes that occurred in myself were an inevitable part of being in action and doing the work, whether internal or for my business, the result of which is I became a better version of myself, living my ideal life.

This growth wasn't always easy. A lot of the time, especially in the beginning, I would lose motivation as I couldn't see immediate results so I'd get discouraged. That being said, the driving force and what kept my focus was I wanted to better myself. Every time I became discouraged I'd refocus and get back on the horse. As I did the work, that got easier and I got better at doing it. Sometimes I was so focused in the work that I couldn't observe all the changes that were occurring in me. Where I did see change was how colleagues, clients and friends gave me more attention, work and respect. I remember a few years back a friend commented on how much I had changed from the prior year. It felt good to know that's what people were seeing on the outside. While I was aware of the change because of small breakthroughs (tasks being easier to accomplish and getting the results I wanted), I didn't know the totality of who I was becoming. That realization came later when I looked back and saw where I came from. I had leveled up as a person.

This is a journey to the summit of success. The most important aspect I had to learn about was myself, who I was, what were my innate qualities and what skills did I need to work on in order to grow. I question myself often about what information and skills I have and what I need to learn in order to show up better every time. This quest for information, like change, allows me to be open to new ideas, testing and trying them to see what works for me. The more awareness I have about myself and my work the better I am able to plan, work smarter and grow. It is an endless process that brings contentment, joy and certainty in myself. No good project should ever be complete. It should be constantly worked on and tweaked. The best project I can think of is growing and developing myself. I hope you think that of yourself too.

I will leave you with a quote :

"Do. Or do not, there is no try"
- Yoda

SELF WORK: What information or skills do you need to know right now so you can move forward?

APPENDIX

Meditation Mantras

Repeat these phrases in your mind:

I am a money magnet.
Money follows me everywhere I go.
Every breath I take, the more money I make.
Money finds me, everywhere I go.
I deserve all the money people want to give me.
Money is attracted to me, and I am attracted to it.
No matter what I do, more and more money finds me,
every single day.
Money flows towards me effortlessly.

Limiting Belief Grinder:

www.impactfulchangeshypnosis.com

1. What does this belief limit you from experiencing?

2. What emotions are generated by this limiting belief?

3. What emotion(s) would you experience in your life without this limiting belief?

4. If you had not had this limiting belief 5 years ago, how would life currently be different for you?

5. What about 2 years ago?

6. What about 6 months ago?

7. If you conquered this limiting belief today, on a scale of 1 to 10 how significantly would you score the impact?

8. If you lost this limiting belief and could make room for a non-limiting positive belief today as well, how would you score your level of future experiences in 6 months?

9. 2 years from now?

10. 5 years from now?

11. 10 years from now?

12. 20 years from now?

13. Ask your unconscious mind, how have you benefited from this limiting belief?

14. How has this limiting belief been negative for you?

15. How does this limiting belief affect others?

16. In a positive way?

17. In a negative way?

18. If you could flip this belief from limiting to non-limited, from negative to positive, what would it look like when written or typed out?

19. If there was any way to remove this limiting belief from your life, what would that be like for you?

20. If you don't know how to answer the previous question, that is fine. But if you did know, what would it be, what would that look like to you or feel like for you?

21. Since you know you need to now release that negative limiting belief, what is stopping you from that?

22. Could a person or persons help you with releasing this limiting belief? Who and/or what kind of person are they?

23. What would they do to be of service to you as a limiting belief remover?

24. On a Scale of 1 to 10, one being the lowest and 10 being the highest, how painful is this belief?

25. When was the first time you felt this way?

26. Do you now know how to overcome this limiting belief?

Flipping Negative Beliefs:

Belief 1: Why do I believe this?

Flip the belief:

Belief 2: Why do I believe this?

Flip the belief:

Belief 3: Why do I believe this?

Flip the belief:

Belief 4: Why do I believe this?

Flip the belief:

Belief 5: Why do I believe this?

Flip the belief:

Belief 6: Why do I believe this?

Flip the belief:

Belief 7: Why do I believe this?

Flip the belief:

Visualizing Your Business Goals

Starting or growing your company:

1. What are you selling? Is it a product or a service?

2. What is that product or service? What are the offerings? If you have a few options, what are they? Why do people need your product/service?

   If it's a product, where are you getting it, do you have a design? If it's a service, how are you going to do it? Answer in detail.

3. Do you have a logo? What are the colors of the logo? How does it look?

4. Do you have a website? How many pages do you need on your website? (I find a 3 page website is pretty good to start - an about us, offerings page, and contact page.) About us - how did this company come into being? Why do you exist? Offerings - use what you wrote above in #2.

5. Who is your target client? Give a full description of who they are and why they need your product/service.

6. How will you reach your clients? Where can you advertise your product/service? What do you need to say in your advertisement to get people to reach out and purchase the product/service? What is your message?

Visualizing Your Business Goals

Getting a promotion or a new job:

1. What is the new job or promotion you want?

2. What skill sets do you need for the job, do you have them? If not, where can you learn those skills? Is there a school or online?

3. What steps are needed to get to that space so you can get that job? Answer for both mental and physical.

4. Who do you need to talk to? Maybe you need to talk to someone in the company about what you need to be qualified. Maybe you have a friend who works in the industry and can give advice. Or you met someone at an event. They might have a job for you or give you information to help you to get that job.

5. These questions are all very very important to make sure you're getting noticed. What additional effort do you have to put in? Is there a way to stand out from everyone else?

6. Do you need to leave your company for a new one to get a promotion?

Matthew Gros-Werter - Author, Businessman, and Meditation Practitioner. His journey is one of continual growth and improvement, driven by a relentless pursuit of becoming faster, better, and smarter in both his personal and professional life. Seeking guidance from mentors and teachers, he has absorbed invaluable insights to propel his endeavors forward.

As a spiritual seeker, Matthew has embraced meditation as a transformative practice, integrating its principles into his daily routine and business endeavors. Meditation serves not only to calm his mind but also as a tool to navigate challenges, conquer fears, and enhance critical thinking. Through this practice, he has honed his ability to think quickly and critically, fostering the development and implementation of innovative concepts that have significantly improved efficiency and his business acumen.

With a portfolio of businesses under his ownership and a track record of successful consulting engagements, Matthew specializes in sales and marketing strategies. His expertise and strategic insights have driven tangible results, establishing him as a respected figure in the business world. Matthew's journey exemplifies a harmonious blend of spirituality, mindfulness, and entrepreneurial prowess, making him a noteworthy figure in both personal development and business circles.

Made in the USA
Middletown, DE
15 October 2024

62599761R00076